AF486674

A Breath Away ...

Vida

A Breath Away

Copyright © 2024 Priyanshi (Vida)

All rights reserved.

DEDICATED TO

Him & I -
And Our Secret Midnights

A Breath Away

Every night I prayed to die,

Then I realized,

Death wasn't the end of existence,

Death was the absence of life,

So, I had died long before that time.

Death is not the end of life but itself a part of life.
It is the moments of sitting on the bathroom floor, with your hands on your mouth to muffle your screams and eyes shimmering; with your friends in a coffee shop and feeling a sense of detachment, it is being in the arms of your lover and feeling foreign. Death is not the end but parallel to life, sometimes one is bolder than the other, and that defines the moment.

So, all of us who live every day do die, and that is the beauty, but the miserable are them, who merely exist, experiencing neither the smile of sunshine nor the tears of midnight.
Melancholy surrounds when one has neither loved nor lost, neither fallen nor stood up, neither committed a mistake nor learned. I feel pain for them, it's just that their journey to themselves is harder than ours.

It is not the end,
Just a moment,
And that is the beauty and tragedy of death.

Death is not always sad and gloomy with grief but the moments of utter peace and serenity.

It is walking in the park with your mother at night, talking about all you both believe about love. It is those Friday nights when you sit with your father and share a drink. It is the moment with our siblings late at night with our playlist on, while we are busy reading. It is early morning conversations with our pets on their walk. Death is in brief moments.

So, I appeal to the Court of Humanity, to amend the notion of death and free it from all the negativity burdened on it, it equally deserves to be loved and cherished; remembered and written.

Because if we repeatedly tell Death how ugly and unworthy of love it is, then one day like us, it will also lose its hope and light, and I won't be able to endure one more shimmering soul to perish, so I appeal to you.

He asked me what it was to have someone he lost,

I replied with pain in my heart
"You want to hear the truth or the lie?" ...

An unexpected answer rolled away from his soul:
"Surprise me"

So, I told him that it would be a mix of lies and truth...

I explained the two sides of the coin

He asked me on which side did I belong,
I kept quiet...
I promised him to answer it someday
How can a person take a stance when she herself has
lost the line between the truths and the lies...

Perhaps, the surprise is the truth to be remembered...

Why do we symbolize grief, pain, and death with the colour black?

Yes, I agree, that it makes us feel emotions we never knew existed, but it is not to be scared of. From what I see, black is the colour that signifies depth, passion, and strength while simultaneously bringing light to vulnerability and feelings. When all the colours of life- beautiful and brightening- come together they form black, so it can be rightly said that black is not the void in our soul but the most colourful art of the soul.

Black is not loneliness but rather solitude and peace. It is not the hopeless future but the midnight shimmering sky, alarming us of the upcoming dawn, Black is not the colour of failure, it is very much the symbol of strength and enlightenment. So, all of you who are attracted to this special colour not because of its aesthetic but because of an unknown energy pulling you towards it, don't be afraid; as light came into existence only because there was dark. So, embrace it and flow along, you surely will discover every other colour along the journey.

If you are tired of the fleeting life, hold on to death; it shall never leave your side, even if you try to.
It will hold onto your skin leaving its mark deep into your soul. It will paralyze you at midnight and take your breath in daylight. It will make you paint the sceneries no one has ever dared to look at, it will make you write poems of feelings no one ever had the courage to share; it will make you do the impossible.
It will always stay by your side, accompanying you, whispering in your ears- beauty isn't soft and weak; it is power and grace. Death will make you up and then tear you down and continue doing so until you bloom into a black rose, swaying against the wind.

We all read how uncertainty is beautiful but deep inside you and I crave and wish our lives were a book, so we could flip through a few of the pages and see how everything ends. It's the truth no one accepts even to themselves, and it is terrifying how we all reach a point in our life, blinded by the colours of life, painted by someone else that we start rejecting our own feelings and opinions, and enter denial. If we could deny, we are so cruel to ourselves that we would deny till covered with sand and still not accept how broken we were, how much we wanted to cry, how miserable everything was because in this world no one cares about the black rose … you don't care how sad the little girl in your skin was.

Maybe my healing was never peace but vengeance,
But the older I get,
I realize it was neither of them, but
Just an apology from them.

I saw my young self,
In my father's lap
Beside my beautiful mother
Smiling like the moment will last forever

And here I am
18 years after
Suffering from my mental disaster
Forgetting how to smile truthfully

I cry seeing my young self
So peaceful, so calm
Unknown of the upcoming pain, love, and magic
I cry because now I feel
Every time I have cursed myself,
I have cursed that little kid
Who is smiling at me, so innocently That, now
I can only imagine and picture
What my real smile looked like.

So, I think
With time
I did not lose just my childhood
But also,
my soul...which I would never find even if I could...

Today I have a question for the rule makers of the world.

Answer me the greatest of lovers, why was love symbolized by light and brightness when all it is, is a trial of time? When all love is the trial of passion and pain, why is it rainbows and unicorns and not forests and blood?

A soul broken into halves named them soulmates and condemned by the lords of the world to separate. The broken halves scattered in different forms and corners, forming the universe. Life is nothing but a long-lost journey to find our way back to our soulmates and let the two halves collide and become the stars, guiding other soulmates with their light on their way to find their better half. Love is nothing but this journey to become stars- and that is how the world works- on love and nights.
Love is the dark corners of our soul which becomes less scary when holding hands of our soulmate. Love is the possessiveness to keep our companion close to us till eternity and beyond. Love is the pain to think of a life without our significant other, and hope in life when all is just fear. So, tell me, darling, am I not right to call love dark - signifying our broken souls and dried tears, touched by an equally broken being? Reigning the depths together.

For me, love is a poem written with passion with black ink and pages stained by tears and kisses and stored in the safest places and read with the utmost respect. I beg the lovers of the world; to let at least love show its darkness and not succumb to the colour you painted our eyes with.

Let love breathe …

I am sitting under the naked sky,
bearing my deepest desires.
He is covered with stormy clouds, with wind on its
command but
at the nook, there is a glint of gold,
which is his heart...fading with every passing second.
His eyes have spelled everyone,
and his whispers have made every soul shy ... But
he is standing there with command and no emotion,
I beg him, to bear his feelings even if it is hatred for
us...for me...
I will take anything he is willing to give.

And all of a sudden, the leaves stopped whispering
the wind stopped swaying,
and the music of the flowers died,
That's when I looked up and realized,
he was gone...forever...in the darkness of secrecy
and I couldn't save him, I couldn't hold onto him,
like every other being.
Once again, we were just a mere spectator to the
disappearing beam of light,
and then, they ask me why I love darkness.
It took my love whom I couldn't hold in my
arms
and tell that I was there
and would die in his memories

It's midnight as I realize that every moment is death, every moment is an end because it will never happen again.
You will never read this page again for the first time, you will never again shout your favourite songs at midnight to suppress your loud doubts, and you will never smile at yourself the way you did today, what am I even saying- you will not be your present self ever again… that somewhere puts my mind to rest that I will never have to live my pain again but only my soul knows that parting with my pain is also hurting, letting go of my tears is somewhere leaving me emptier than I can make peace with. So, I realize that I was not made of stardust to perish and become part of the mighty universe, I am made of pain and memories, and when I perish, I will be carved in the pages I bled on, will be lost between the lines of the songs I smiled at and will be forgotten from the memories of the person I died for.

I am not here to ask you darling to remember me but beg you to forget me, so I can cry for you, and maybe I will feel complete again.

Forget me…

I talk of death
When the sun rises and sets
I feel death
When I wake up and sleep
I crave death
When I stand alone
I believe in death

But,
Somewhere,
Life pulls me toward itself
With a force unknown
Maybe it is my father's embrace
Or my mother's eyes
It can also be my dog's little lies
Or my darling's wishes

Maybe death is my soulmate,
But life is my lover.

Can end and forever coexist? I hope that one day when "you &I" end, "us" stays forever.

 I hope one day when I have long passed away, you find my torn pages, where I have written my feelings for you, where I have confessed my love for you a thousand times, where I have shared my deepest desires for our future…I hope you find those pages, so you will remember that someone is always beside you. Someone truly loved you. Even if death already met my prayers, always remember that I will be holding your hands, drinking your tears, and decorating your smiles, for my existence revolved around life and death - you were my life and death was my fate.

I know that we won't ever end up together in any of our lifetimes - our love would never cross time and space, but I am just contented to know that our departure will. I know you will never remember me, but I am just contented to remember you, I know you will break my heart into a million pieces, but I am just contented to meet death with those broken pieces…

I know, I know, I know…but still this flickering hope inside me makes me wonder of all the what ifs, If I can take my last breath with your hands around mine and your tears falling for me. I will be at peace.

Hope is the greatest enemy of acceptance…

I will not walk into your life,
Because the day I swore to love you
Was the day I swore to keep you smiling.

The sweetest and the most painful death is to die in someone's memories.

To die in yearning. Death is a journey. The journey to feel his kiss when you close your eyes but encountering the raindrops upon realize. It is to imagine how you could have a small cottage by the lake, poems on the walls, pictures of you both by the bedside stand, his smell across the home, and a heart to feel your own. It is to live in the memories that were never created, tears that were never spilled, and smiles that were never received. It's so painful… him to be your entire world and you to be nothing in his world… it aches but tell me what is love without ache, what is death without hope.

I cried for him every summer night because he said that no one ever loved him. I feel pathetic myself for not being perfect for him and stand and shout out to the world how much love for him stays submerged in my heart…this is death.

I smiled for him every fall afternoon when he came to my cafe with a beautiful girl for a date and whispered sweet little words to each other…this is death

I took him home when he was drunk but he kissed me by the moon … and I was taken aback wondering if the universe unmasked my unspoken wishes … But then he called her name … yet I continued to feel fortunate…this is death

I met him after a decade, but he did not remember my name…yet I continued to feel the butterflies upon seeing him again …this is death

I realize every moment I ever shared with him was just a long journey to death and nothing else… yet I continued to write about him…this is death…

23

I am happy I did not confess
Because then how could have I deceived you with a
friendly smile
My only chance to make you smile for me

Your hand is there
I wish to grab it
I wonder how warm it is
I wonder how many promises are sketched
I wonder if they fit with mine
But just it has a ring
With an initial that engraves his heart,
And sure, it's not me,
Because I could never bring myself to make a way to his heart,
Because I never wanted to feel the real,
so, I decided to live in delusion...
A lie yet beautiful

She looks at you with so much love,
I wonder if I ever did,
Then I remembered,
you were not a picture for me
But every fibre of my soul.

Death is crying for your younger self.
Death is when you realize that the world and you were not fair to your younger self. It is crying for the fact that you were so hard on her. You cursed her so much. You loaded her with so many expectations when all she wanted was to see the world. Death is losing your younger self. You could have loved her for what she looked like. You could have loved her for the mistakes she made for the first time. You could have loved her when her heart broke for the first time. You could have loved her when she thought of suicide. You could have loved her… you could have been there for her … when everyone left, and she realized that you were just like everyone who left.

She was young, she was innocent; she carried the burden of your parents, of your siblings, of your friends but never once she sat with herself. She cried at midnight when you slept peacefully.

All our younger selves were stronger than we could ever be, they were better liars than we could ever see- their moist eyes and trembling lips. They were a better being than us.

I beg your pardon, to show sympathy to her, to let her go of all the mistakes that she never meant, to all the times she could never hold, let her fly … at least after her death.

She is long gone… perished into the moonlight. I can't imagine she was seventeen and in love with death. She was so young when she prayed for her end. I can't imagine how hard it was for her to live, just for you.

I . beg . you . with . every . breath . of . my . life… don't forget her. She was the most enchanting soul who once lived.

So, I assume we will feel familiar with our demise because it will be the second time. Even during the end, she made sure that we wouldn't feel alone when the time comes.

She grew up,
Year after year,
Learning how to hide her.

But I am searching for the spark,
The smile that would stretch wide,
The giggles which would make my grave feel light.

The fingers soft with the fairies and dragons,
The small arms which held the world,
The angel who fell.

I am searching her in the shell the world carved,
I am searching Me in the eyes that were never ours.

Year after Year I grew,
Never finding who I was,
Never finding where she was.

Maybe this was the story of my red thread
Her lost in me,
Me, lost in her,
Falling for each other.

A Breath Away

DEAR READERS

As we come to the end of this memory lane, I really wish that a part of you feels unleashed. A part which you have hidden for too long comes alive and makes you feel again. I understand that the emotions which might be swaying in your tightened chest might be hurting but I promise, it will be alright. My darling readers, I request you to never numb your emotions, let the waves wash over you, because the tighter you will hold on to the more it will pain, the more you will suffocate and in a million years I pray that you never feel strangled by your memories, never feel breathless from your tears. So, find yourself in these verses, and remember the universe is there for you, I am there for you praying that every broken piece of you lightens and shines like the stars.

Thank you so much for staying till the end of this book. You all make me feel so cherished and content that I am incapable of expressing that gratitude through words. Thank you for all your love and support and I hope I was able to touch that beautiful soul of yours.

Love You All.
With Gratitude,
Vida

ABOUT THE AUTHOR

Vida, is a young writer, embarking on her literary journey with her first book "A Breath Away … ".

She loves to write about the stories which never made it to the end. Her love for writing about the beauty she sees in the darkest of corners and about love which was never spoken of continues to grow with every passing day. She wishes that every person who reads her work finds a piece of their hidden self.

Currently living in the Indian city of Bengaluru, our young writer loves to spend her time - reading, listening to songs, painting and writing her favourite ideas on her blog. Her never wavering excitement to get into discussions which are deep and philosophical makes her feel enriched and content in life.

Connect with her on:
Instagram - @vida.priyanshi
Blog - priyanshivida.wixsite.com/lunallovizna

ACKNOWLEDGEMENT

I want to express my heartfelt gratitude to every reader who has embraced this book. Your support and engagement have given purpose to my writing journey. To my family, thank you for your unwavering belief and encouragement. Mom, Dad, Yash, and Rapy, your comforting presence during the emotional highs and lows of this project means the world to me.

My gratitude extends to my friends and well-wishers whose conversations and support have often sparked inspiration— some of which you may even recognize within these pages.

Lastly, I extend my deepest thanks to Him—my love, my muse, and the moon I admire. Your constant presence, attentive ear, and belief in my words have been my greatest source of strength.

I also want to express gratitude to the universe for allowing me the opportunity to translate my emotions into words that may offer solace to others.

Thank You All for being the part of this journey.

A Breath Away

33

www.ingramcontent.com/pod-product-compliance
Lightning Source LLC
Chambersburg PA
CBHW051420130726

47989CB00007B/3011